Looking at Countries

INDIA

Jillian Powell

W
FRANKLIN WATTS
LONDON·SYDNEY

First published in 2006 by
Franklin Watts
338 Euston Road
London NW1 3BH

Franklin Watts Australia
Level 17/207 Kent Street
Sydney NSW 2000

ISBN: 978 0 7496 6478 7
Dewey classification: 915.4

Series editor: Sarah Peutrill
Art director: Jonathan Hair
Design: Rita Storey
Cover design: Peter Scoulding
Picture research: Diana Morris

Picture credits: All photographs Dinodia Photo Library except for the
following: Binder/Superbild/A1 pix: front cover inset, 27.
Superbild/A1 Pix: front cover main, 11, 20, 26b. Every attempt has
been made to clear copyright. Should there be any inadvertent
omission please apply to the publisher for rectification.

A CIP catalogue record for this book is available from the British
Library.

Printed in Hong Kong

Franklin Watts is a division of Hachette Children's Books.

Contents

Where is India?

India is a large country in Asia. It is the seventh largest country in the world.

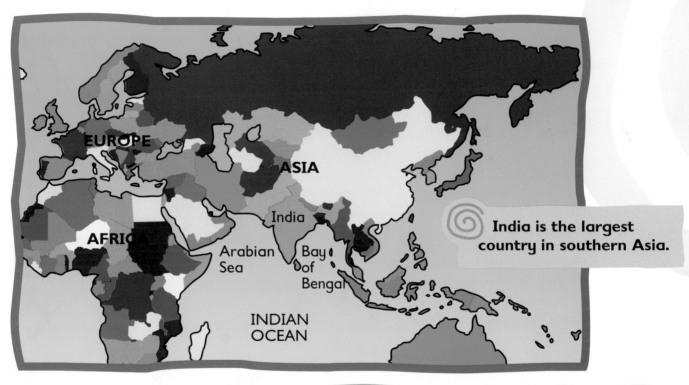

EUROPE

ASIA

AFRICA

India

Arabian Sea

Bay of Bengal

INDIAN OCEAN

India is the largest country in southern Asia.

India's capital city, New Delhi, is in the north. It is an important business centre, with offices, banks, factories, shops and an international airport.

These large buildings in New Dehli have government offices inside.

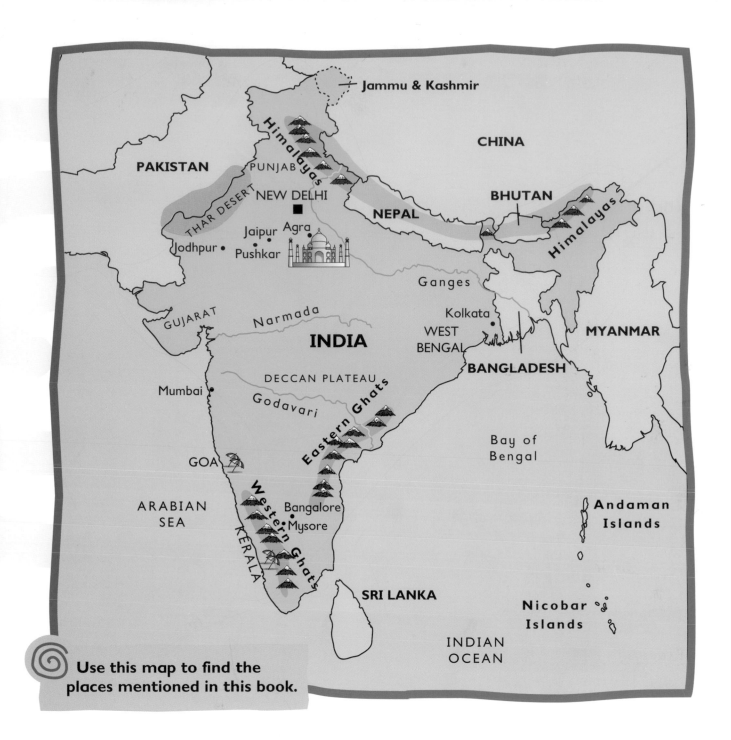

The map shows:

Jammu & Kashmir, CHINA, Himalayas, PAKISTAN, PUNJAB, NEW DELHI, THAR DESERT, BHUTAN, NEPAL, Himalayas, Jaipur, Agra, Jodhpur, Pushkar, GUJARAT, Narmada, INDIA, Ganges, Kolkata, WEST BENGAL, MYANMAR, BANGLADESH, DECCAN PLATEAU, Mumbai, Godavari, Eastern Ghats, Bay of Bengal, GOA, Western Ghats, ARABIAN SEA, Bangalore, Mysore, KERALA, Andaman Islands, SRI LANKA, Nicobar Islands, INDIAN OCEAN

Use this map to find the places mentioned in this book.

Did you know?

People in India call their country Bharat.

India has a long coastline along the Arabian Sea to the west, the Bay of Bengal to the east, and the Indian Ocean to the south.

The landscape

India has a varied landscape. In the north are the snowy Himalayan mountains, which have some of the highest peaks in the world.

The tops of the Himalayas are covered with snow all year round.

Across the middle of the country is a huge, flat plain crossed by three great rivers, including the Ganges. Most of India's people live and work on the fertile farmland there.

Did you know?

Tigers still live in the wild in India's jungles.

Fields of mustard plants are common in the Punjab – a dry region on the border with Pakistan.

Along the border with Pakistan is the dry Thar Desert, where little grows. Further south is the high, flat Deccan Plateau, and either side the forested mountains of the Eastern and Western Ghats.

India also has many beautiful sandy beaches, especially in the western states of Goa and Kerala.

Beaches like Vagator Beach in Goa draw tourists from all over the world.

Weather and seasons

India has three main seasons. The cooler winter months last from October to February. Summer follows, with hot, dry weather bringing drought to many parts of the country until June.

These women are collecting water during a drought in Gujarat on the west coast.

During the monsoon season, there is heavy rain every day.

Then the monsoon season starts. Warm winds blow in from the Indian Ocean, bringing heavy tropical rains that flood the streets. During the monsoon, there can be fierce storms called cyclones. These bring high winds and tidal waves to the east coast.

The Himalayas in the north have the coolest temperatures in India. The hottest temperatures are in the Thar Desert, which can reach 45 degrees Celsius in the summer heat.

Did you know?

Many Indian songs and poems celebrate the arrival of the monsoon rains.

Indian people

Over a billion people live in India, more than in any other country, except China. Each state has its own language, costume and traditions. Religion is important to Indian people. They say prayers every day, and live their lives according to the rules of their religion. Most people are Hindus but others are Muslims, Sikhs or Christians.

Did you know?

Three major world religions – Hinduism, Buddhism and Sikhism began in India.

Hindu homes have family shrines for daily prayers.

In the town of Pushkar, people speak Hindi, Rajasthani, English and Gujarati. These women are shopping at the town's market.

Hindi is the main language, but there are 18 other state languages and over 1,600 different dialects. English is used for business and government. Children usually learn Hindi, English and their state language in schools.

School and family

Children in India start school when they are 6 or 7 years old. There is free schooling for all children until they are 14 years old.

The children at this primary school in West Bengal have to line up in classes before the start of lessons.

But many children from poor families do not go to school or only go for a few years. They have to work to bring in money for their families. The poorest are children who live on the streets and beg for money.

Relatives share a family celebration at an Indian home.

Family life is very important in India. Often children, parents and grandparents live together in the same house. Family celebrations and religious festivals are a time for relatives to get together.

Did you know?

When women in India get married, they usually go to live with their husband's family.

Country

Most people in India live in the country. Many farm small plots of land, growing enough to eat, and sometimes a little to sell or swap at market. They keep cows for milk, and use oxen or water buffaloes to pull farm carts.

Did you know?

Cows in India sometimes have their horns painted to show which family owns them.

Most work, such as sowing and harvesting crops, is done by hand. Children help with farm work and jobs such as fetching water from the village well.

A boy washing himself with water taken from a village well.

Some people make crafts, such as cloth or baskets, and sell them at markets to bring in a little money.

Street sellers use bicycles to carry and sell goods from village to village.

City

Cities in India have grown fast as young people have moved in from the country to find work. The capital, New Delhi, is a busy city with many businesses and also the country's main government buildings.

A street in New Delhi, decorated for a festival.

Bangalore is a high-tech city, with IT companies and research centres. Mumbai, India's largest city and port, is an important centre for trade and industry.

Did you know?

Mumbai used to be called Bombay.

This street in Mumbai is full of traffic.

All India's cities share problems of over-crowding, poverty and pollution. Roads are packed with cars, scooters, buses, trams, lorries and bicycle rickshaws.

Although rich people enjoy a modern lifestyle with shopping, restaurants, health clubs and nightlife, many people live in poverty without jobs, homes or healthcare.

Indian homes

Many city people live in modern blocks of flats. The richest people have big houses with gardens and modern equipment such as air conditioning and satellite television.

Did you know?

Jodhpur is called the Blue City because many of its houses are painted blue.

This brightly-painted house in Mumbai is a fisherman's home.

These modern blocks of flats are in Jaipur.

The poorest people live in slum houses made from scrap board or metal. They do not have clean running water, which can cause health problems.

These slum homes in Mumbai are next to a railway track.

These traditional village houses, in the region of Gujarat, are built from mud and straw with palm thatch roofs.

Many traditional village houses are built around a courtyard, where there is a shrine for daily prayer. Often, a family lives in one big room, with a storeroom and a shelter for their animals.

Food

Most Indian food is colourful and spicy. People like to shop for fresh foods and spices from local markets.

Did you know?

The dish called Bombay duck is really fried fish!

There are many different sorts of spices on this market stall in Mysore.

Spicy vegetable stews and sweet milk puddings made with nuts and spices are popular everywhere. In the south, stews are eaten with rice, or served with rice cakes or rice-flour pancakes.

In the north, dishes are often served with flat bread such as *parathas* and *chapatis*. Many Indians eat no meat because they are Hindus. Muslims eat no pork.

This woman is cooking chapatis outdoors in an Indian village.

At home, Indians often eat meals sitting cross-legged on the floor.

Many families enjoy meal times together, sharing several dishes of different foods such as rice, spicy vegetables and yoghurt.

At work

India has industries such as farming, fishing, textiles, machinery, chemicals, aircraft, cars and computers.

Did you know?

Bangalore is known as Asia's Silicon City because of its fast-growing technology industry.

The manufacture of cars is one of India's growing industries.

The tourist industry brings millions of visitors from all over the world to visit India's bustling cities, beautiful beaches and famous buildings such as the Taj Mahal.

Workers in a call-centre take lots of calls all day.

Service industries such as call-centres, banks, mobile phone companies and travel companies are growing fast, providing more jobs for women workers.

In the country, most people work in farming, using simple hand tools and water buffaloes and oxen to help them. Millions of village children help on farms, and others make or sell goods, to bring in a little money for their families.

A man in the region of Gujarat herds his animals using a long stick.

Having fun

In the cities, many people enjoy going to the cinema to watch the latest 'Bollywood' film, made by Mumbai's film industry. At home, richer families have satellite or cable television.

Did you know?

More films are made in India each year than in any other country.

This Bollywood film poster is advertising a comedy.

Director's Special 123 Hits presents

NOMEETA SANDHU'S

EK SE BADHKAR EK

Deepak   Gulshan   Sunniel   Raveena   Shekhar

co-producers VIRENDER DHINGRA PAMAL ARORA written by DILIP SHUKLA music by ANAND RAAJ ANAND lyrics by DEV KOHLI action by SHYAM KAUSHAL cinematograph by AN

A group of young women throw coloured powder (gulal) for the spring festival of Holi.

Hockey is India's national sport.

There are many colourful religious festivals through the year, such as the Hindu festivals of Divali and Holi. People celebrate by dressing up, feasting, dancing and watching firework displays.

Sport is popular in India. Hockey, cricket and football are played everywhere and are popular sports to watch with regular games and events. Traditional sports such as elephant and camel racing, and team games such as *kho kho*, a chase game, and *kabaddi,* are also popular.

India: the facts

- India is a republic and a member of the Commonwealth of Nations.

- It is the largest country in South Asia. The President is the head of state and the Prime Minister leads the government.

- India is made up of 28 states and 7 territories that each has its own government. The territories include some of the larger cities and islands such as the Andaman and Nicobar Islands.

The Indian currency is the rupee.

- India has the second highest population in the world, after China.

The Indian flag has orange, white and green bands with a Buddhist symbol at the centre. Green stands for a rich land, white for peace and orange for courage.

The Taj Mahal in Agra is one of
India's most famous landmarks.

• The main cities include the capital
New Delhi, Mumbai, Kolkata (once
known as Calcutta) and Bangalore.

Did you know?

The Taj Mahal was
built as a tomb for a
dead Empress.

Glossary

Bicycle rickshaw a small vehicle for passengers pulled by someone riding a bicycle.

Call-centre a centre where workers answer telephone calls from customers.

Commonwealth of Nations a group of independent nations that were once ruled by Great Britain.

Dialect a language or way of speaking in a particular region.

Divali the Hindu festival of lights and New Year, which is held in October or November.

Drought a long period without rain.

Fertile rich and productive.

Head of state the main representative of a country; sometimes the leader of the government.

Holi a spring festival in northern India.

Jungle a tropical forested area.

Kabaddi a team game that combines wrestling and a sort of rugby.

Monsoon seasonal winds carrying heavy rain.

Plain a low, flat area of land.

Plateau a high, flat area of land.

Pollution dirt in the air or on the land caused by chemicals from traffic or industry.

Republic a country with no king or queen, where decision-making power is held by the people and their representatives.

Shrine a place where people pray.

Textiles cloths or fabrics.

Tidal waves huge waves caused by high winds or earthquakes.

Traditions ways and beliefs that have been passed down through generations.

Find out more

http://home.freeuk.net/ elloughton13/india.htm
This website has a section for children aged 7–9, to give them an insight into the diverse culture and landscape of India. For each part there is a 'slide show', a bedtime story, somewhere to keep 'notes' and suggestions for other websites to explore.

www.timeforkids.com/TFK/hh/ goplaces [click India]
A guide to India with famous sites, a history timeline, some phrases in Hindi and a day in the life of an Indian child.

Note to parents and teachers: Every effort has been made by the Publishers to ensure that these websites are suitable for children, that they are of the highest educational value, and that they contain no inappropriate or offensive material. However, because of the nature of the Internet, it is impossible to guarantee that the contents of these sites will not be altered. We strongly advise that Internet access is supervised by a responsible adult.

Some Hindi words

Hindi is the national language of India. It is spoken by about a third of all the people and understood everywhere. It is written in a different way from English with a different alphabet.

English	Say
excuse me	su-ni-ye
hello/goodbye	na-ma-ste
market	baa-zaar
my name is	me-raa naam [your name] hay
no	jee na-heeng
please	kri-pa-yaa
thank you	thaynk-yoo
yes	jee haang

Some Hindi words used in the English language
Bandanna – head band
Bangle – bracelet
Basmati – type of rice
Chintz – cotton cloth
Chutney – fruit or vegetable pickle
Jodhpurs – trousers for riding
Juggernaut – large lorry

My map of India

Trace this map and use the map on page 5
to write the names of all the towns.

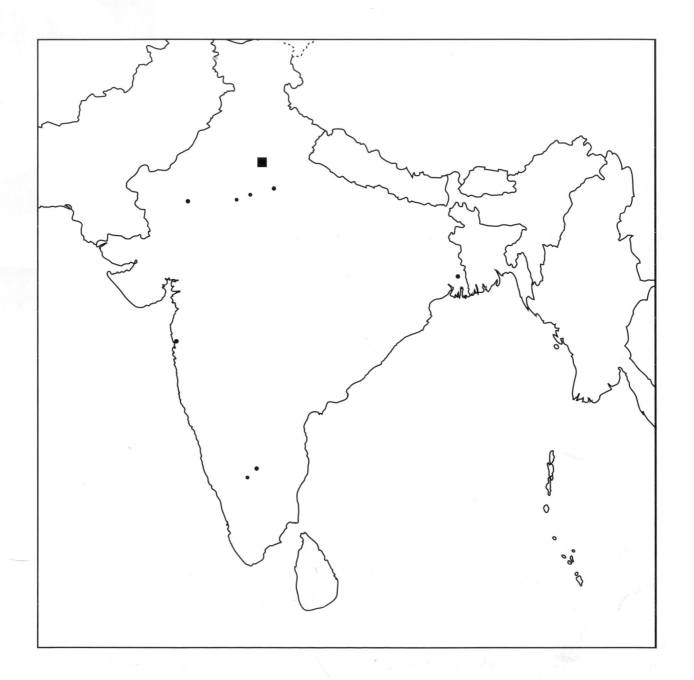

Index